The Oxford Centre for Staff Development

Learning to Teach

ASSESSING STUDENTS' WORK

Training Materials for Research Students

WITHDRAWN

David Baume and
Carole Baume

Published by
THE OXFORD CENTRE FOR STAFF DEVELOPMENT
Oxford Brookes University
Gipsy Lane
Headington
Oxford
OX3 0BP

Learning to Teach: Assessing Students' Work
ISBN 1 873576 47 1

British Library Cataloguing-in-Publication Data. A catalogue record for this book is available from the British Library.

Designed and Typeset in 10.5 on 14 pt Palatino and Helvetica by Ann Trew
Illustrations by Bob Pomfret

Printed in Great Britain by
Oxonian Rewley Press Ltd
Oxford

Printed on paper produced from sustainable forests.

Contents

Introduction

Remember being assessed? Remember thinking, as you worked and revised and sweated through the course work and the examinations, 'It's all right for the lecturers...'?

As you start doing some assessment, hang on to that memory of being assessed. Remember the experience, the particulars of the assessment you undertook. And remember how it felt to be assessed. These memories will give you a vital empathy with the students with whom you are working and whom you are assessing – even as your sympathy for the assessors increases!

Aims and overall learning outcomes for this booklet

This booklet aims to help you carry out well, efficiently and with moderate confidence any assessment of student work which may form part of your teaching duties.

(Assessment is taken here to mean both giving feedback and marking.)

Section 1 deals with marking. It should help you to use and, where necessary, clarify and construct the marking schemes which are intended to assure comparability of standards in assessment.

Section 2 is intended to help you give good, clear, useful feedback to students on their work, and to do so in a way that doesn't make huge demands on your time.

Section 3 aims to explain some of the basic ideas which underlie good assessment practice. It should help you make sense of information on the syllabus and objectives or learning outcomes and assessment criteria for your course, and assist you in applying this information as you assess.

Section 4 endeavours to help you prepare students for assessment, by helping them to make sense of assessment.

Assessing Students' Work

Marking

M arking is the crunch.

You're a good, bright, well educated, supportive tutor. You have the best interests of your students at the forefront of your attention. You care. And then you have to put a number or a grade on their work.

In doing so, you will directly affect whether they can take the subjects they want next year, or whether they pass to the next year at all, or whether or not they graduate.

You have on the desk in front of you a pile of their work. You also have the exam paper or project outline or whatever brief they were given. Hopefully, too, you have some kind of marking scheme to show where the marks should be allocated or withheld. And there's you, and your judgement, and your responsibilities to the students and to the course and the subject and the university. What do you do? How do you proceed?

Aims and learning outcomes for this section

This section is intended to familiarise you with the basic principles of marking student work and to give you some practice in doing so. It should also help you to work with marking schemes devised by others, and, where necessary, to clarify or even devise marking schemes of your own. In addition, its purpose is to assist you in developing a little confidence in your ability to mark in a rigorous and professional way.

On completing the section, you should be able to mark student work in your subject area in a way which conforms with good marking practice and the formal requirements of your university, department and course.

1.1 Marking: some basics

1.1.1 Introduction – marks for what?

You need as much clarity as possible about what you are awarding marks for. That's what much of this section is about.

You may have to dig for this clarity. Having got hold of the project specification and the marking scheme, you may still need to ask further questions. Most lecturers would rather be doing research than assessing, or even thinking about assessment. Some would rather be cleaning out the drains.

Why this reluctance to think about assessment? Without going deeply into the psychopathology of assessment, one reason is that lecturers know that assessment shows how well they have taught, in addition to how well the students have learned. You may need to persist to get the clarity you need!

1.1.2 Scales and standards

What marking or grading scale will you be using – percentages, A–E, 1–16, some other?

What standards are applied?

There are two ways to approach these questions.

- One is to ask what each point or each band on the scale actually means, in terms of the nature, quality and maybe quantity of work.

- The other is to ask what the distribution of marks or grades should be – roughly what proportion of scripts should fall into each mark or grade band.

(We'll explain later, in Section 3, why we prefer the first approach to defining standards over the second.)

1.1.3 Your role in marking

Will someone else also mark the work? If so, how will any differences between their mark and yours be reconciled? Are you expected to make comments on the report or script? Will your comments be seen by another assessor, the student's tutor, the student? Will you be required to attend the assessment board, and perhaps defend your marking?

What other questions do you have about your role in assessment?

Who knows the answers?

What are the answers?

1.1.4 Analysis or overview?

You could start by giving an overall mark to a piece of work, based on an overall impression, and then do a detailed analysis against the marking scheme. Alternatively you could start by awarding marks for each part of the answer according to a marking scheme, and then seeing if the resultant mark feels right.

Whichever way round you work, you know you are getting better at marking when your impressionistic and analytic marks start to agree.

1.1.5 Subject differences

You will need to adapt what is said here to the particular needs of your subject. Take advice! For example, science and engineering can have more precise and analytic marking schemes than arts subjects.

1.1.6 Above all, seek help

We can't say this too often: ask for help and advice from more experienced colleagues about marking. They may find your questions uncomfortable. Their answers may not be as clear or helpful as you'd like. Ask anyway.

Marking

1.2 Marking schemes

A marking scheme (similar to, and sometimes called, a model answer) shows how marks are allocated. Here is an examination question, and its associated model answer/marking scheme.

1.2.1 An example

The question is taken from a BTEC Higher Certificate in applied biology (Habeshaw et al., 1993, pp. 120–21).

Question	Marking scheme (marks in brackets)
Determine the rate of growth of bacteria in two different feeding media.	
a) Plot the data on a single side of graph paper and in the most appropriate manner. (12 marks)	a) Graph: (total 12 marks) Title: (Growth (0.5) of a bacterium (0.5) in two media (0.5) at 30°C (0.5) with aeration (0.5) X-axis: time (0.5); hours (0.5); sensible scale (0.5) Y-axis: counts (0.5); volume (0.5); log plot (0.5); sensible scale (0.5) Plots: correct plot for each set of data (2); sensible line for growth pattern for each set (2); zero time count calculated (2)
b) Calculate the mean generation time of the bacterium in the two media. (2 marks)	b) Mean generation time (total 2 marks) 2 values within 10% of correct answer (2)
c) Explain why the innoculum was washed and predict the likely result of the experiment if the innoculum had been taken directly from a nutrient broth culture. (4 marks)	c) Explain/predict (total 4 marks) To remove nutrient broth from innoculum (2); no lag phase in nutrient broth (1); growth rates of cells in defined medium would be different (1) OR any other sensible suggestions (1)
d) In this experiment, colony counts were used to determine the increase in population size during the incubation. Suggest another method which could have been used to measure the increase. (2 marks)	d) Another method (total 2 marks) Absorption (2) OR any other reasonable suggestion (2).

Even a marking scheme as apparently precise as this leaves some scope for judgement by the assessor, as signalled by the words 'correct', 'reasonable' and 'sensible'. But, if they knew the official 'correct' answer, different assessors would be likely to give the same answer similar marks.

Here is a very different marking scheme, a more general one, for a dissertation (adapted from Gibbs et al., 1992, p. 15).

a Clear statement of the focus/area/topic/problem/hypothesis (10 marks)

b Substantive review of the relevant literature; good relation of theory and literature to the actual research being undertaken (10 marks)

c Justification of the research topic, setting and programme (10 marks)

d Choice of appropriate research method, setting and programme (10 marks)

e Clear description of the research method, setting and programme (10 marks)

f Appropriate and sufficient collection and clear presentation of data (10 marks)

g Thoroughness of critical analysis and evaluation of the research, with clear and detailed reference to data and to literature, appropriate theories and explanations, and some appraisal of validity and value (10 marks)

h Sensitivity to problems and processes of research undertaken, e.g., ethics, communication, negotiation, collaboration and dissemination (10 marks)

i Substantial conclusion, raising key issues and points, with suggestions for future research/practice as appropriate (10 marks)

j Full, accurate bibliography; appendices as appropriate (10 marks)

Although less precise, this still gives good guidance to a marker. (It would also give good guidance to the students preparing their dissertations: more on this in Section 4.)

1.2.2 What if there isn't a marking scheme?

You could persuade the person who set the examination to produce one. There really should be a marking scheme for assessments where the results contribute in any way to students' final assessment! Or you could write your own. It's difficult to give advice in writing marking schemes which apply across all subjects, but the following pointers may help.

- An outline marking scheme is better than none at all – it doesn't have to be as detailed as the one above to be useful.

- If yours is a subject where there are right and wrong answers, decide what proportion of marks should go to getting the right answers and what proportion to each step of the argument or calculation.

- Do put into the scheme '... or any other reasonable solution'. There's usually an answer or an approach which is OK but didn't occur to you as you wrote the marking scheme.

- If your subject doesn't have a lot of right answers, there are still features you'd expect in a good answer: sources you'd expect to see referred to, arguments you'd expect to see clearly made, chains of reasoning you'd expect to see followed. Decide what weight to give to each of these.

- Get some reactions to your proposed marking scheme from the course leader or another lecturer on the course. Don't be surprised if they ask you for a copy!

Marking

1.3 Working through the pile

1 Read, and assign a tentative grade to, the first five scripts before you start marking. This will give you a feel for the overall standard.

2 Skim through the scripts, just sorting them very impressionistically into, say, five grade piles (for example, A, B, C, D, E, or whatever grading system your institution uses).

3 Alternatively, try to put them all into rank order, then work out where the grade boundaries lie. Check a script from either side of each boundary with an experienced tutor.

4 Mark all the scripts.

5 When you've finished marking, check back with the first five you marked to make sure your standards haven't drifted up or down as you mark.

6 Draw a few scripts at random from the piles and mark them again. Check with your original mark. Again, have your standards changed? Why?

To give each student the appropriate mark, you need to make sure your marking standards are consistent from once piece of work to the next. You also need to make sure you are marking to the same standards as your colleagues. This needs practice and continued conversation about assessment.

1.4 Practising using a marking scheme

This exercise should help you to develop the skills of assessment before you have to do it live.

1 Get hold of:

- a recent project briefing or examination paper – whatever kind of work you will be marking – from your course and subject

- the marking scheme, model answer, or whatever guidance was provided for assessors

- the course syllabus and handbook

- department and course examination requirements and regulations

- one or two pieces of assessed student work made in response to the brief or question (preferably without examiners' marks written on them).

2 Mark the work against the marking scheme. Pretend it's for real.

- As you mark, note any difficulties you have. (Most of these are likely to revolve around the question of how many marks to award for what, and how to cope when the student's answer is different from the marking scheme but still possibly OK.)

- When you've finished marking, compare your marks with those of the original assessor.

- Explore, and try to resolve from the paperwork you have, any discrepancies.

3 Politely but firmly ask for a few minutes with the course leader or assessment tutor. Talk through with them what you have done. Show them the difficulties you've had. Ask them how they would have dealt with these and how they would have marked the work. They'll be impressed as well as, we hope, helpful.

4 Repeat steps 1 to 3 until your marks are within 5 per cent or half a grade (e.g., B/B+) of the original assessor's and you feel confident in your ability to mark.

1.5 Administering assessment

Because assessment is a serious business, it is often undertaken very formally. This gets truer the nearer you approach to the board at which assessment decisions are formally taken.

Your course, department and university will have assessment regulations and procedures. Marks will need to be presented in particular ways, on particular forms or spreadsheets. Scripts will need to be handled in particular ways, on specified time-scales, sometimes in particular envelopes placed in specified trays or cupboards. These requirements are to ensure security for the students' work and confidentiality about the marks until they are confirmed at the examination board. Course leaders like assessors who are reliable, which here means doing what's asked of them, however odd the procedures seem.

Giving Feedback

Feedback is essential for learning

This whole pack stresses that learning is an active process. Learning is far more than simply 'being taught'. To learn, we need to plan what we're going to do; attempt to do it; and then receive feedback on our work. We then use this feedback to improve the work we have just done, or, more often in education, to ensure that the next work we do embraces what we have learned. This account of learning as a cyclical process is considered further in 'Powerful Ideas in Teaching and Learning'.

Your own research almost certainly reflects this cycle of learning and the place of feedback in it. First, a meeting with your supervisor to review your recent work and plan the next phase. Next, long hours, probably alone, in which you do the work, sometimes as planned, sometimes with accidental or planned deviations. Then a further meeting to describe what you have done, debate it, receive comments and suggestions, and plan the next phase.

Undergraduates can learn well in much the same way. Much (sometimes too much) of the planning is done by the tutor rather than by the student. But, for the learner, the feedback remains essential. They may snooze through the odd few minutes of your lecture or seminar, but they will read, pore over, analyse, debate, argue with, and quite possibly treasure, your feedback. This section should help you to give feedback which merits such intense attention from your students.

Giving good feedback is a skill which can be learned and honed. It is a valuable skill in most professions, and indeed in most aspects of life.

Aims and learning outcomes for this section

This section is intended to persuade you of the importance to student learning of good feedback.

It should help you to:

- react positively to good things in students' work

- make helpful suggestions on ways in which their work could have been improved, assist in correcting misapprehensions revealed in their work, and advise on how they can change their approach in the future

- do all this in a way which respects the individuality and worth of each student and which makes good and efficient use of your time.

2.1   The feedback sandwich

Not surprisingly, the Open University has done a lot of work on giving useful feedback to students. (By 'useful' here, we mean feedback which meets the needs of the learners and the obligations of the course and the tutor.)

The Open University recommend the feedback sandwich:

- first, the good news

- then the bad news (constructively!) and how to overcome it

- and finally, a high note of encouragement.

We also recommend this approach to giving feedback.

2.2 The good news

2.2.1 What and why?

Students need to know what they've done right, or well. They need to know this so that they'll keep on doing it right or well, and also because it will make them feel appropriately good about themselves and their work, which in itself aids learning as well as feeling good.

What phrases could you use to tell a student they had done good work in your subject?

How would you feel if you received feedback like this on your work?

Students may also need to know why their work was right or good. Learners sometimes do well by accident – so tell them in what respects it was right or good.

What phrases could you use to tell a student why their work was right or good in your subject? (You'll need to be more specific than you were above. If you get stuck, think about feedback you received, or would like to have received.)

2.2.2 Giving good news

Good news needs to be:

- clear
  Don't beat about the bush. If you think it was 'great' or 'excellent' or 'admirable' or 'very stimulating', then say so. Have the courage of your convictions. (Don't worry about using cliches!)

- specific
  Words like 'great' or 'excellent' carry a strong emotional message, but when the emotional buzz fades, the intellectual hunger remains. As we suggested above, say what, exactly what, was good and say why it was good.

- personal
  Make the person to whom you're giving feedback feel acknowledged as an individual. This will become easier as you get to know your students. Using their name in the feedback helps – *'Emma, I thought the way you handled this was both valid and original. I particularly liked the way you ...'*

- honest
  As well as being truthful, honest good news also clearly distinguishes between fact and judgement. A numerical answer is 'right'; fact. A design was undertaken 'rigorously'; opinion, though based on clear criteria for rigour. An argument was 'original'; fact, at any rate relative to your own current knowledge. An argument was 'elegant'; an opinion, or at any rate a judgement. Be clear what the nature of your good news is.

Assessing Students' Work

2.3 The bad news

2.3.1 What and why?

Students need to know what they've done wrong, or poorly, or whether they have performed in some other way which is inappropriate within the subject. And, immediately and always, they need to know in what respects their work was wrong or poor or inappropriate. They also need suggestions on ways in which it could have been correct or better.

In primarily numerical or scientific disciplines, where at least some of the answers to some of the questions can be right or wrong, reasons for giving prompt and reasoned feedback on wrong answers include:

* so that the learner won't repeat the specific error

* so that they can identify the misunderstanding which led to the error

* so that they can develop a new and correct understanding.

In disciplines where answers are more likely to be considered good or bad rather than primarily right or wrong, reasons for giving this kind of feedback on poor answers include:

* to help the learner appreciate why their approach or answer was inappropriate

* to help them see the preferred approach

* to help them see why the preferred approach is preferred.

Make notes on a representative error or poor answer in your subject.

Draft some possible feedback to the student on their poor answer.

How would you feel if you received feedback like this on your work?

2.3.2 Giving bad news

Bad news needs to be:

* specific — Make it clear what you are reacting to – which word, which idea, which equation, which stylistic feature. Explain in what respects the work is wrong, inappropriate – whatever it is.

* constructive — Suggest how the work could have been made accurate, good, to conform to the paradigm of the subject, whatever. Suggest sources of information and guidance. Give the student a handle, encouragement, whatever seems right.

* kind — Specific is kind. Constructive is kind. 'Poor' scribbled at the bottom is cruel.

* honest — See above under 'Good news'.

2.4 Encouragement

Round off your feedback with a high note and encouragement.

'You really seem to be getting to grips with this'

'Your analytic skills are improving steadily'

'You're making good use of evidence'.

2.5 Feedback on your feedback

Add to these lists of what feedback should be like. You'll develop your own style. Ask the students whether they're getting from you the feedback they want and need. Delighted to be asked, they will tell you!

2.6 Giving feedback more efficiently

Students greatly value feedback on their work. Feedback is individual attention, an individual response. Your carefully considered comments on their work, your suggestions on how they could have tackled it differently, your suggestions for a particular piece of further reading which casts important new light on the topic – all these will be very well received.

The trouble is, you probably don't have an hour or more to spend giving feedback to each student on their work. How can you make sure they get quality feedback without you staying up all night providing it? There are several ways.

2.6.1 Feedback from themselves and each other

The final part of Section 4 of this booklet explores student self- and peer assessment. It talks about these as ways of preparing students for being assessed. You can also use self- and peer assessment to get feedback to students.

Self-assessment – how can students give themselves feedback?

Get the students to **answer questions** about some work they've just done. Good questions include:

'What are the best features of this piece of work?'

'How could it be improved?' and

'What would have made it one grade, or say 5 or 10 per cent, better?'

Tell them the **assessment criteria**. Do this before they undertake the work! Then, when they've finished, ask them to write a few comments on how well they think they've met each of the assessment criteria.

When they've done the work, give them a **marking scheme**, and ask them to mark their own scripts. As a result of doing this they will have feedback on what features of their work were good, poor or missing.

A similar approach is to give them a **model answer**, again when they've done the work. They can use this to see what they're doing well and less well in comparison with your idea of a fine answer.

Peer assessment – how can students give each other feedback?

Peer assessment works in pretty much the same ways described above for self-assessment. Students rapidly become good at giving each other feedback, especially if it's structured in the ways we're suggesting here.

2.6.2 Feedback from you

Your students will still want some feedback from you. And quite right too.

You could give them feedback on audio tape, recording your immediate reactions as you read through their work, rather than a carefully considered response after you've finished reading. This gives them feedback quickly, personally, directly, and cheaply.

You can try this alternative if you set the same assignment last semester or year, or if another lecturer has set it previously. List the ten or twenty comments, corrections, observations which you're most likely to make in giving feedback on this work. Write them up as a numbered list. Add space at the top for the student's name, course, assignment name. Print off as many copies as there are pieces of work to assess. Now you can 'give feedback by numbers'! On the list, tick the comments which apply to the piece of work you're marking. Or, a bit more sophisticated, place the number of the comment alongside where it applies in the student's work.

This gets individual feedback to each student. It saves you the need to write out the same comments lots of times. It leaves you some time to make individual comments on errors or strokes of brilliance which aren't on your pre-printed list. It also leaves you more time for your research. An example of an assignment attachment form is provided on the next pages.

Psychology Practical Comment Sheet

Name: .... Date Submitted: ....

Practical: .... Mark: ....

Marker: ....

Checklist of Comments

TITLE
( ) Missing ( ) Correct ( ) Incorrect ( ) Vague ( ) Too short ( ) Too long
( ) Incorrect but adequate

ABSTRACT
( ) Needs the heading "Abstract" or "Summary" ( ) Section missing ( ) Too short
( ) Too long (max. 200 words) ( ) Unclear
( ) Wrongly placed, it should be at the beginning
( ) Omits hypothesis/aim - design procedure results - conclusion
( ) Material which is here belongs elsewhere, e.g.
( ) Clear ( ) Succinct

INTRODUCTION
( ) Section missing ( ) Heading missing
( ) Too short (min. 300 w) ( ) About right length ( ) Too long (max. 1,000 w)
( ) Follows handout too closely ( ) Rambling and unfocussed
( ) Does not incorporate a statement of the hypothesis
( ) Rationale for study missing
( ) Does not review previous empirical findings ( ) Omits relevant readings
( ) Does not consider appropriate theories
( ) Some material included here belongs elsewhere, e.g.
( ) Inappropriate use of references ( ) Well argued
( ) Shows set reading has been done

METHOD
( ) The entire section is missing ( ) Should be sub-divided as below:

Subjects
( ) Number? ( ) Groups? ( ) Sex? ( ) Age? ( ) Naive to purposes of study

Materials/Apparatus
( ) Section missing ( ) Not enough detail ( ) Too much detail
( ) Needs diagram

Design
( ) Section missing ( ) Control(s)? ( ) Balancing? ( ) Randomisation?

Procedure
( ) Section missing ( ) Instructions to subjects? ( ) Details missing
( ) Too detailed ( ) Whole section clear and detailed

Results
Tables
( ) Missing ( ) Summary table needed
( ) Calculations/Raw data go in Appendix
( ) No numbers/titles on tables (e.g. "Table 1: Mean errors for each age group")
( ) Untidy ( ) Neat

Figures/Graphs
( ) Missing   ( ) Axes need labelling   ( ) Key to symbols? ( ) Wrong items plotted
( ) Bad scaling on axes   ( ) No numbers/titles on figures (e.g. "Figure 1: Graph of")
( ) Untidy   ( ) Neat

Description of Data
( ) Missing   ( ) Too short   ( ) Good length   ( ) Put some of this in Discussion

Statistics
( ) You have not done all the tests described in class
( ) Link this with a table/result.
( ) Arithmetic errors   ( ) Tables/figures neat and well presented
( ) Verbal description clear/precise

DISCUSSION
( ) Missing   ( ) Little evidence that you have done the required reading
( ) Too short ( ) Too long
( ) Mention problems with procedure/design
( ) Does not pick up points raised in the Introduction
( ) Conclusion missing ( ) Your conclusion is not justified from the data presented
( ) Material has been included here which would go better in the Introduction
( ) Satisfactory   ( ) Well organised   ( ) Well organised and well argued
( ) Contains some novel and interesting opinions

REFERENCES
( ) Some references are incomplete
Minimum information is :
(a) first author (b) title of article or book (c) title of journal (if relevant)
(d) volume number (e) year of publication   (f) publisher (books only)
( ) Some references made in report are not detailed here
( ) Some references are inaccurate
( ) Section missing   ( ) Satisfactory

GENERAL
( ) Poor ( ) Fair ( ) Good   ( ) Very good   ( ) Excellent
( ) Too brief overall   ( ) Too hurriedly written
( ) Report not set out in formal order
( ) Poor spelling   ( ) Poor grammar   ( ) Untidy
( ) Difficult to follow your arguments: muddled, disorganised
( ) Too long (you need to demonstrate skill in condensing your argument)
( ) Overall presentation above average
( ) Demonstrates reading beyond set references and extra marks have been
   awarded for this

This sheet is one of series prepared by the Psychology Unit, Oxford Brookes University, and is reproduced here with kind permission of Dr R Paton and Dr S Fearnley.

Aims, Outcomes & Criteria

Assessment is an important, and therefore often an emotionally highly charged, business. Where marks and degrees are at stake, it is often also a complex and bureaucratic pursuit, stiff with regulations and even rituals.

In the middle of all this, one vital question can sometimes be given insufficient attention. That question is 'What is being assessed?'

Good practice in higher education, as in any education, tries to answer this question at three levels.

First, accounts are given of overall **course aims**, of what the course is trying to achieve.

Next, more detailed course **learning outcomes or objectives** are developed. These describe, in more or less detail, what the students will need to show that they can do in order to pass the course.

Finally, some courses also adopt **assessment criteria**. These describe what makes a good or a less good answer. They are used, sometimes together with marking schemes, to suggest what characteristics of a piece of student work should lead to the award of what class of mark or grade.

Aims, learning outcomes and assessment criteria are important parts of the language and good practice of assessment.

Aims and learning outcomes for this section

This section will introduce some important concepts in assessment. It will also help you to become comfortable in using these concepts to analyse and clarify assessment tasks before you start to give feedback to students, mark student work and prepare students for assessment.

By the end of the section you should feel justifiable confidence in your ability:

- to recognise and distinguish between course aims, learning outcomes and

assessment criteria in your subject area

- where necessary, to clarify aims, learning outcomes and assessment criteria

- to plan how you will make appropriate use of learning outcomes and assessment criteria as you give feedback to students on their work, mark their work, and help them to prepare for assessment.

3.1   What are course aims?

Look back to the statement of the aims of this section. This should have given you a rough idea of what to expect. It says that the section is an introduction, and does not claim to offer the last or even the middle word. It mentions giving feedback, marking and preparing students for assessment. It also says what the section should do for you – help you become comfortable in using the concepts.

In short, this statement of aims should have helped you see what this part of the booklet is about, what it is for, before you start to work your way through it.

The statement of aims for the course you are teaching should similarly assist you in giving an overview of the purpose of the course to the students. The course leader or a lecturer should already have done this, but do it anyway. You will give a different angle, and you will also be able to get a sense of what the aim means to the students, which will greatly help your work with them.

You should return to the course's aims at intervals during the course. For example, there you are, working deep with the students in a problem on some tricky technical item, and someone (quite possibly you) wonders how what you're doing relates to the course as a whole, to the big picture. You can go back to the course aim, a lighthouse which should be visible even over the largest waves of a rough sea.

3.2 What are learning outcomes?

Learning outcomes are derived from aims. Aims are general statements of what the course is about, what it is for, what it is intended to achieve. Learning outcomes spell out that aim in much more detail.

In brief, the learning outcomes of a course are what the student has to show they can do in order to pass it.

The learning outcomes for this section are that by the end you should feel justifiable confidence in your ability:

- to recognise and distinguish between course aims, learning outcomes and assessment criteria in your subject area

- where necessary, to clarify aims, learning outcomes and assessment criteria

- to make appropriate use of learning outcomes and assessment criteria as you give feedback to students on their work, mark their work, and and help them to prepare for assessment.

Considerably more detailed than the aim, these learning outcomes should tell you what you should be able to do by the end of the section.

Good learning outcomes contain a lot of verbs describing student actions, actions which should be public and testable (for example, describe, distinguish or analyse rather than appreciate, explore or understand).

Not all courses contain learning outcomes as we've defined them here. Some academics think it's inappropriate to specify learning outcomes in this way, perhaps because they feel it reduces education to the level of mere training. Others agree that it's a good idea to specify them but haven't got round to it yet. Still others have started to do it and found that it's difficult. However, increasingly, the tendency is for course learning outcomes to be specified in this kind of detail.

3.3 What are assessment criteria?

Assessment criteria are derived from learning outcomes. Learning outcomes are what you have to achieve in order to pass the course. Assessment criteria describe how, how far, how well.

We haven't specified assessment criteria for these booklets – after all, you're not going to be assessed, or, if you are, not through these booklets. But, to help us work on this topic, what sort of assessment criteria might apply to you on this section of your training? In other words how, how far, how well, should you have to achieve the first two learning outcomes we suggested for this section in order to be fit to practise as a tutor in your department or school?

By the end of the section you should feel justifiable confidence in your ability:

- to recognise and distinguish between course aims, learning outcomes and assessment criteria in your subject area

- where necessary, to clarify aims, learning outcomes and assessment criteria.

The first learning outcome for this section presents few problems.

What would be an appropriate assessment task for this learning outcome? We could ask you to look at some statements about a course, and say which of them are aims, which are learning outcomes, which are assessment criteria, which are borderline cases and which are none of the above. We'd be happy if you could do this correctly (i.e., in a way that agreed with us!) say 80 per cent of the time. (Other assessment criteria for this objective, and certainly other acceptable success rates, would of course be possible. Assessment criteria are scarcely ever right; they are merely agreed as reasonable.)

Assessing Students' Work

The second learning outcome is a little more problematic. Who decides where clarification is necessary? Presumably, you, the course leader and/or the students.

How do we judge the success of the clarification? The course leader and the students would certainly have views on how acceptable your clarification would be. They would judge from rather different points of view. The course leader would judge to what extent your attempt at clarification was accurate. The students, though still of course interested in accuracy, are less able to judge this. They will, however, have strong views on the success of your attempt at clarification!

In case it all seems a bit abstract, look at it this way. Assessors do make decisions on how many marks a piece of work is worth. You may feel more secure, both as an assessor and as someone helping students prepare for assessment, if you can talk clearly and openly about the basis on which assessment judgements are made by you and by your colleagues on the course.

3.4 Clarifying learning outcomes and assessment criteria

You may feel that the learning outcomes or assessment criteria for your course are expressed less clearly than we are suggesting here is desirable. If you do, then there are several ways to clarify them. Look at past exam papers and other assessment tasks to see exactly what knowledge and skills are being tested. You'll also need to look at marking schemes, perhaps also at the reports of the assessment board, and at external examiners' reports. You can of course talk to the course leader, other lecturers on the course, and your mentor.

The question you are trying to answer is 'What do students have to do to pass, and, beyond that, to get particular grades or marks?' (Your colleagues may not like this stark phrasing of the question. Use your judgement and your diplomatic skills.) But the clearer the answer you can find to this question, the better you can achieve the third of the learning outcomes for this section, the ability to make appropriate use of learning outcomes and assessment criteria as you give feedback to students on their work, mark their work, and and help them to prepare for assessment, and the greater the justifiable confidence you will feel in your ability to do so!

3.5 Working with learning outcomes and assessment criteria

Later sections of this booklet cover how learning outcomes and assessment criteria should inform your work as you give feedback, mark students' work and prepare students for assessment. But before that, some final comments which apply to all you do on student assessment.

1   Keep learning outcomes and assessment criteria at the centre of your consciousness as you work on any aspect of assessment. They describe, after all, the basis on which your students will be guided in their future work and marked on their past efforts.

2   Continue to work to clarify learning outcomes and assessment criteria, for yourself and with your students. Learning is a cyclical process. Students (and therefore good teachers) return to ideas several times during a course. At each return, the idea is further developed in light of other things which the student has learned and as the student's own mental model of the subject develops.

3   Continue to work on the relations among the course aims, learning outcomes and assessment criteria. These three elements should be closely interdependent, in the course and also in your and your students' thinking about the course, the subject and the assessment.

Preparing Students for Assessment

The rules of assessment

Assessment in higher education is, among other things, a game.

The lecturers:

1 decide what the students will have to do in order to pass

2 want most of the students to pass

3 aren't supposed to tell the student exactly what they have to do to pass.

The students:

4 want to know what they will have to do to pass

5 know that rules 1, 2 and 3 above are true.

Given this, what rules govern your behaviour in helping students to prepare for assessment? We would suggest that

You:

6 check out local regulations and customs on helping students prepare for assessment

7 help students to prepare for assessment without breaking rule 3.

This section concentrates on rules 6 and 7, informed by the previous five.

Aims and learning outcomes for this section

This section is designed to help you to prepare your students for assessment in a way which is sensitive to their needs and to the norms of the course, department and university.

On completing it you should be able to plan work with students which will:

- ensure that they are clear about the formal assessment requirements of their course

- ensure that they are clear what the learning outcomes and assessment criteria for their course mean

- ensure that they can relate these outcomes and criteria to the tasks they are set and the work they produce

- help them, in preparation for being assessed, to gain experience at making assessment judgements on their own and each other's work.

4.1 Clarifying the formal assessment requirements

4.1.1 Regulations

The section on marking encouraged you to check out the assessment regulations of your course, department and university so that you can work within them. We re-emphasise the point here. Get hold of the regulations. Then work through them and see what they mean for the students. Don't try to memorise them. Just know, broadly, what they cover and what they say.

4.1.2 Requirements

As well as regulations there with be lots of assessment requirements – for example, for projects there will be hand-in dates, required formats, obligatory cover sheets and the like. Students will expect you to know what they are. Again, get hold of a copy. Again, don't try to memorise them.

4.1.3 Answering student questions

A student asks you, 'If I fail one of my modules this year but get at least a B in the rest, can I still do my current selection of modules in the third year?' Do you work through the regulations with the student to find the answer, investigate and answer such questions yourself, or refer the questions or indeed the student to the module, year or course leader?

Your briefing to teach on this module should have dealt with this issue. If it didn't, ask.

A student asks you, 'What's the hand-in date for this piece of work?' You should know the answer, or be able to find it within seconds.

In general, be cautious in answering the more complex questions about assessment regulations and requirements. Anything you say on the subject may be taken down by the student and used, not necessarily entirely accurately, later.

4.2 Clarifying learning outcomes, and their use, with students

Getting a clear view of what a learning outcome or an assessment criterion means takes time. (You may already have discovered this, as a student and as you worked through the first section of this booklet!) So, don't plan to spend one whole session with your students working on outcomes and criteria and assume that will do it. Spread the work out through the course.

4.2.1 At the first or second meeting of the class . . .

- Draw their attention to the section of the course guide, handbook or syllabus where the learning outcomes are listed. Say something like: *'These are the things you will need to be able to do at the end of the course to pass.'*

- Talk them briefly through the work you did, in the first section of this booklet, on clarifying for yourself what the learning outcomes meant. They'll be interested in your personal account, and impressed and reassured by the thoroughness of your preparation.

- Give them some examples of what the learning outcomes mean. For example, say, *'Here is a question from last year's exam which I reckon tested this outcome.'*

- Ask them if they have any questions about the learning outcomes.

- Reassure them that you'll keep on coming back to the learning outcomes during the course.

4.2.2 . . . And during the course

- Routinely start sessions by saying something like: *'Today the work we're doing relates mainly to the following course outcomes ...'*, and then refer to them in the course handbook and read them out.

- If you are setting student work, talk through how it relates to one or more of the course outcomes. *'You'll see that, once you can answer questions like this correctly, you've achieved most of outcome 4.'*

- Encourage and support discussion on what the current learning outcome means and how it relates to the session. This is excellent preparation for assessment.

4.3 Clarifying assessment criteria, and their use, with students

Once the students start producing work, in the class or between classes, you can start similar work on the assessment criteria. This can lead to fascinating and important discussions.

For example: *'To obtain maximum marks the essay must be within 10% of the specified length, and must provide a **comprehensive overview** of the **main debates** around the topic, leading to a **definite** and **well reasoned conclusion.'***

> *How could you help students clarify for themselves what this account of the assessment criteria for an essay might mean?*

Apart from encouraging them to find out how the word-counter works on their word processor, you could hold lively and productive discussions on the meaning, within the course, of each of the emphasised words or phrases in the sentence. (You should prepare for this discussion by having the same discussion with someone experienced at teaching the course.)

4.4 Helping students make assessment judgements

When they assess, assessors learn almost as much about assessment as they do about the students and what they have learned. You can use this fact to help your students prepare for being assessed by doing some assessing for themselves. For example:

- Before they do a piece of work get them to discuss, and write down, exactly what the assessment criteria should be. They could do this as a group, or in pairs or small groups within a large group.

- Get them to read, make comments on, and perhaps even mark, one another's work. Then encourage them to discuss the feedback and the marks they have given one another. (They won't need much encouragement!)

4.5 Letting them practise!

Every year, students do less well than they could in assessment for reasons that have nothing to do with their knowledge of the subject. They answer the wrong number of questions on the paper. They don't notice that some questions carry more marks than others. They 'describe' when they should have 'analysed' or 'compared and contrasted'.

You can help your students avoid such traps by having one or two sessions in which they practise being examined. In a hour they can at least plan how they'd answer a three-hour examination, or they can answer one question. Then, review with the students how they did.

4.6 Self- and peer assessment

A really good way for students to learn about assessment is for them to do some assessing.

Assess what? Their own and each other's work.

Here are some approaches to using student self- and peer assessment to help prepare students for being assessed. The approaches form a sequence, starting simply and getting more sophisticated. In using these you can employ some of the group techniques suggested in the booklet on tutorials and seminars, especially in the section on large groups.

4.6.1 Good news, bad news

Give each of the students a short piece of work (real, maybe from one of last year's students, or simulated) on the topic. Ask them what they think is good about it and what they think is bad. Get them to work on this alone, then in pairs, then in bigger groups, finally pooling their conclusions for you to write up in public. This is usually a lively and very productive exercise. You can use it to good effect in the first two or three weeks with the group. It's a fine icebreaker!

4.6.2 Devising a marking scheme

Tell the students what marking schemes are (perhaps using Section 3 of this booklet), and show them an example. Give them an example of the kind of question they could be asked to do on the course, or, even better, tell them about a piece of work they're actually going to be doing in the near future. Then, informed by the

previous exercise and using the same sort of group method, get them to devise marking schemes. Discuss them. Try to agree one.

4.6.3 Using a marking scheme

The next step you can take is to get hold of some answers to the question you worked on in the previous activity. Get the students to mark them using the marking schemes they devised. They should do this in pairs or threes. Write up the marks each small group awards. Then get them to explore, perhaps after remixing the groups, the reasons for any discrepancies in their marks (there will be discrepancies!). The discussion will again be lively.

4.6.4 Devising assessment criteria

After all this you can usefully encourage the students to go beyond marking schemes, which are specific to one question, to assessment criteria. As the earlier section of this booklet on learning outcomes and assessment criteria says, 'Assessment criteria are accounts of the characteristics of student work which, at this stage of the course, will attract particular sorts of marks or grades.'

4.7 Final comment

'Should I really be giving all this emphasis to assessment?'

It seems to us that students care a lot about assessment. But there's another, to us very important, reason for working explicitly with students on assessment. In discussing what makes a piece of work in good or less good, you're surely dealing with the very heart of the subject. Assessment is, in the best possible sense of the term, an academic business, and a very proper topic for discussion between tutor and students.

These books and chapters will give you further information and ideas on marking and giving feedback to students on their work.

53 Interesting Ways to Assess your Students

Sue Habeshaw, Graham Gibbs and Trevor Habeshaw. Bristol: TES, 3rd edn, 1993. ISBN 0-947885-12-9.

A book of hints and tips and ideas worth trying for yourself, to dip into rather than read from start to finish. Chapters cover essays, objective tests, computer-based assessment, exams, on-the-spot assessment, log books and portfolios, projects and practicals, feedback to students and involving students in the assessment process through self- and peer assessment.

Assessing More Students

Graham Gibbs with Alan Jenkins and Gina Wisker. Oxford Centre for Staff Development, 1992. ISBN 1-873576-14-5.

Practical guidance, with lots of examples. Chapters include students' and lecturers' experience of assessment, assessment strategies – front-ending assessment, doing it in class, self- and peer assessment, assessing students as groups, mechanising assessment and cutting down on assessment and feedback.

Chapter 4, 'Assessing students', in *Preparing to Teach*

Graham Gibbs and Trevor Habeshaw. Bristol: TES, 1992. ISBN 0-947885-56-0.

Chapter sections on what lecturers say, straight advice and quick tips (about assessment), setting questions, objectives, criteria, marking report sheets, second marker's sheets and commenting.

Chapter 6, 'Assessing the students', in *A Handbook for Teachers in Universities and Colleges: a Guide to Improving Teaching Methods*

David Newble and Robert Cannon. London: Kogan Page, 1991. ISBN 0-7494-0512-0.

A very lively and practical guide, with examples and cartoons.

Strategies for Diversifying Assessment

Sally Brown, Chris Rust and Graham Gibbs. Oxford Centre for Staff Development, 1994. ISBN 1-873576-23-4.

Other publications available from the Oxford Centre for Staff Development

TEACHING MORE STUDENTS

1 Problems and course design strategies
2 Lecturing to more students
3 Discussion with more students
4 Assessing more students
5 Independent learning with more students
6 Supporting more students
Video: Teaching More Students

COURSE DESIGN FOR RESOURCE BASED LEARNING

Course Design for Resource Based Learning in Social Science
Course Design for Resource Based Learning in Education
Course Design for Resource Based Learning in Technology
Course Design for Resource Based Learning in Accountancy
Course Design for Resource Based Learning in Built Environment
Course Design for Resource Based Learning in Art and Design
Course Design for Resource Based Learning in Business
Course Design for Resource Based Learning in Humanities
Course Design for Resource Based Learning in Science
Institutional Support for Resource Based Learning

LEARNING IN TEAMS SERIES

Learning in Teams: A Student Guide
Learning in Teams: A Student Manual
Learning in Teams: A Tutor Guide

DEVELOPING WRITING SERIES

Essential Writing Skills *(in print 1996)*
Using Data
Writing Reports
Scientific & Technical Writing *(in print 1996)*
Essay Writing
Tutor Manual

DEVELOPING STUDENTS' TRANSFERABLE SKILLS

STRATEGIES FOR DIVERSIFYING ASSESSMENT

BEING AN EFFECTIVE ACADEMIC

ASSESSING STUDENT CENTRED COURSES

IMPROVING STUDENT LEARNING – THEORY AND PRACTICE

IMPROVING STUDENT LEARNING – THROUGH ASSESSMENT AND EVALUATION